Selling With H.E.A.R.T.

> **The Only Way To sell confidently, connect deeply, and grow your business with integrity!**

By **Tom Jackobs**

DISCLAIMER

This publication is designed to provide accurate and authoritative information in regard to the subject matter covered. It is sold with the understanding that the publisher and author are not engaged in rendering legal, accounting or other professional advice.

ISBN: 978-1-304-55972-2

SELLING
— WITH —
H·E·A·R·T

THE ONLY WAY TO **SELL**
CONFIDENTLY, CONNECT DEEPLY,
AND **GROW YOUR BUSINESS**
WITH **INTEGRITY!**

TOM JACKOBS

Thank You

A very special thank you to my good friend and coach for over 15 years, Camelia Ruth. Without her "gentle" push, this book would not have been written.

All of my clients who trust me to help them improve their sales. By coaching them it helped me formulate the heart-centered sales framework which is the premise for this book.

My friends and family who have supported me with all of my hair brained ideas and projects.

Dedicated to the memory of my Dad, John Jackobs, who we lost January 10, 2023. He was a lifelong learner and teacher. Through his example I always strive to learn more.

Table of Contents

Foreword

By **Pete Cohen**, Business Coach, Best-Selling Author and Keynote Speaker

www.PeteCohen.com

In a world where authenticity and compassion are at the heart of health and wellness, the word "sales" often evokes a sense of unease. As heart-centered coaches, we are driven by a deep desire to serve, support, and uplift others on their journey to well-being. The notion of selling may seem incongruent with our mission, leading us to question its place in our practice.

In this amazing book, Tom Jackobs explains that sales is not the enemy. In fact, it is an essential tool that allows us to reach more souls and make a greater impact. By embracing the art of selling, we extend our reach to those who are seeking guidance, support, and transformation in their lives.

I have known Tom for many years and not only have I seen him teaching sales, but I've also seen him on the front line selling, and he is someone who totally understands the beauty, the skills, and strategies to be effective at selling. Tom has not only beautifully articulated the power and importance of sales for heart-centered coaches, but he has done so with such grace and eloquence. His words resonate deeply with the essence of our calling, reminding us of the profound impact we can make when we approach sales with authenticity and compassion.

Tom's ability to convey the message that sales is not a dirty word, but rather a means to connect, educate, and empower others, is truly commendable. His writing inspires us to embrace sales as a vehicle through which we can create profound transformations and help individuals embrace a holistic approach to their well-being.

Why I Wrote This Book

I'm an introvert and an empathetic person.

That was the biggest excuse I used as to why I wasn't good at sales.

I used to say things like, "I don't want to push people to buy something they don't want." or "I shouldn't have to push people to purchase, if they want it they will buy."

Perhaps that's hitting close to home for you?

My biggest problem was, using those excuses kept me from growing my business. I almost went broke with that mindset.

Both of those excuses are complete mind trash … and the wrong mindset for those who want to grow their business, especially for health and wellness professionals and practitioners.

Why do we make these excuses?

Why do we have such a bad connotation of sales?

Nothing happens in business without a sale, which is an exchange of value. Sales make or break a business, sales help people, and sales keep us doing what we love to do.

Once I changed my mindset and focused on how I could help people the most, I became a MACHINE, selling well over $10 million dollars — both for myself and for others. I LOVED IT! And I no longer felt bad about it.

Someone once said to me, "You could sell ice to an Eskimo," and I was greatly offended. Why was I offended? Because I would never sell something to someone who didn't need what I was selling!

That is the mindset every health and wellness practitioner needs to adopt.

That is why I'm so passionate about helping "Heart-Centered" practitioners like you increase their business and reach more people … oh … and make more money doing it while maintaining a high level of integrity and unity with their core values.

How would life be different if you believed in your heart what you have to offer … your product or service … would benefit your prospects? You must believe it is your duty and obligation to help them solve their problem with your product or service.

And wouldn't it be great if you never felt like you're selling, but rather, solving a problem?

In this book, which I wrote as a practical *how-to* guide, I will go through the process of selling so you can do it much better. The best part is that it's a ***process***, and when the process is done the same way every time, you will get the same great results over and over again. You will have a growing and thriving business you are proud of.

(…and help tons of people along the way!)

I've written these chapters to give you a better understanding of WHY I do things in a certain way, with clearly defined steps in the sales process. You'll be able to use this book as a guide to refer to over and over again.

I also recommend getting the Workbook that goes along with this book (**www.TomJackobs.com/heart**), so you can design your sales presentation like a pro.

Put your seatbelt on, as you're about to embark on a wonderful journey to helping more people while putting more money in your pocket, and without feeling like you need to take a shower after every sales conversation.

And of course, if you need help along the way, I'm just an email away at tom@tomjackobs.com. In addition, I have tons of resources on my website (www.TomJackobs.com) and my YouTube Channel (www.tomjackobs.com/youtube).

Section 1: H.E.A.R.T.

"Your work is going to fill a large part of your life, and the only way to be truly satisfied is to do what you believe is great work. And the only way to do great work is to love what you do. If you haven't found it yet, keep looking. Don't settle. As with all matters of the heart, you'll know when you find it."

- Steve Jobs

Chapter 1

The Wellness Practitioner and Sales

"I don't feel I should HAVE to sell my service." - every broke wellness practitioner

---

S o many health and wellness professionals I've worked with (myself included) cringe at the idea of "selling" their services. Is that you?

The belief I once had and have heard from many other health professionals is, "I shouldn't *have* to 'sell' my services, people should inherently want it and if they don't buy, they're not my ideal client."

I understand the thought process. I used to think that way too.

The truth of the matter is, most people who NEED your service have a million reasons NOT to buy the solution to their problem. Maybe you've heard these excuses:

- I've tried everything and nothing works

- I don't think I have that condition

- I don't want to make the changes necessary to achieve my goal

- It's too hard

- Just give me a pill

It's your duty to help the prospect realize they have a problem big enough to solve NOW — not tomorrow — now, and with *your* program.

This new approach to selling is what I call heart-centered selling. With heart-centered selling, you are focused on helping solve the problem your prospect has, versus focusing on making a sale. There is a big difference in mindset and how the prospect (and you) will feel about the interaction.

It is through this heart-centered approach to selling that you will be able to overcome limiting beliefs and help your prospect realize they need to make a change, they need to make that change NOW, and they need YOU to help them make that change.

When you approach the sales conversation with your prospects HEART FIRST, not only will they feel how much you care about them and their best interests, you will feel a sense of accomplishment when you enroll them into your program (that's another way of saying "sell them your program"). Most importantly, you will have done it with INTEGRITY and HEART.

When most health and wellness practitioners went through their education, licensing and certification, chances are there was never a course on sales.

What a pity, because this is the ONLY way we help more people, make more money and stay in business. Sales makes business happen, and without it, there is no business and you will have helped no one.

It's as simple as that.

When you master this new approach to sales, you will be unstoppable. Your business will boom, and more people will benefit from your expertise.

You're in an extremely honorable industry. It can truly be life or death for many of your prospects. And if you don't sell, you don't serve. Only sales will elevate your practice.

This is why I always say the following in my workshops and trainings:

It's your duty and obligation to MASTER these skills. And if you don't... You might as well get out of the industry.

Sorry to be so blunt and harsh about it, but it really is that critical. You're in a unique position to drastically change the trajectory of your prospect's life, but only if they enroll in your program.

My heart-centered approach to selling isn't about developing clever "closing" techniques or memorizing objection-handling scripts. It's about finding what the problem is and presenting a solution to that problem in a way that entices your prospects to purchase the solution, transform their lives, refer their friends and give you raving reviews.

You're a Problem Solver

Once you realize that sales is about solving problems, you will be able to sell with a high level of integrity and feel great about helping your prospects.

Once I figured this out in my own fitness and wellness business (Body3 Personal Fitness), I went from a close rate of 10% with an initial sales value of $600, to a 90% close rate with an initial sales value of $5,000 within a matter of 6 weeks. Let's put some real numbers on this.

BEFORE: 10 People asked about personal training, with one person purchasing a $600 package. My total revenue for that sale would equate to $600 for a one and-a-half month period, with no guarantee of future earnings.

AFTER: 10 People had a heart-centered consultation with me about personal training, and an average of nine people bought my $5,000 12-month package, equating to $45,000 in revenue over the next year.

Same number of prospects — drastically different outcome — simply because I changed my own mindset and followed a structured sales process.

I don't want to sound braggadocious with those numbers, it's a demonstration that if I can do it, you can too. I'm not a natural-born salesperson and frankly, I don't believe anyone is! It's a process and a skill that is taught and learned, and then practiced and repeated with amazing results.

All of the clients I've personally coached have at least doubled their sales in six months with the methodology and process I'll be taking you through in this book.

It's not rocket science, it doesn't require an outgoing personality or the 'gift of gab'. It just requires following the process **consistently**.

That's why it's so important to master this skill, and I'm thrilled you're reading this book.

PRO TIP FOR USING THIS BOOK

This book should be used as a guide to create your own personal sales process using the framework I outline. It's not a book you read once then put it on the shelf, but one you should refer to on an ongoing basis so you can truly master the art and science of selling with heart.

Each chapter will build upon previous content with practical ideas and stories to emphasize my points.

The companion workbook will allow you to put what you have learned into practice and further solidify your learning.

FREE BONUS MATERIALS

If you want to go a bit deeper and further solidify your learning, I've put together a companion video course to go along with this book, along with some goodies to help you put what you learn into action.

Simply go to **www.TomJackobs.com/book/training** it's free to use, and my way of building trust in me.

You can also scan this QR Code:

Chapter 2

The Heart-Centered Approach Explained

In my world, heart-centered selling means you are selling with integrity and congruence with your values in an effort to help another person solve a very personal problem.

Many of the professionals I've worked with have a nurturing personality type — which is great for the wellness field, however, it can be in direct conflict with a sales role. The good news is it doesn't have to be.

Nurturing personalities really love community, bringing people together, have a sense of service ingrained in them and are likely to be empaths.

They are likely to be people pleasers and want everyone to like them.

And that can cause some internal conflicts when selling. The hard truth is that not everyone is going to like you and not everyone is a great fit to work with you. I'm sure you've had those clients who had all the right intentions, but were a real handful to work with.

It's ok to let go of those who don't want your help or don't align with your values, and it's ok to have conflict.

When you accept those truths, selling from your heart will be a breeze.

When you're selling from the heart, you're asking deep questions to figure out what the problem is and — more importantly — you're having your prospect verbalize what their problem is so they become aware that they indeed have a problem.

Without a problem, there is no need and without need, there is no sale…

When you approach the sales conversation with a genuine desire to help your prospect solve their problem (and knowing that you can), that is heart-centered selling.

Most of the clients I work with struggle with the parts of the sales process where they have to present their solution. Oftentimes they go into "coach mode" and try to solve the prospect's problem right then.

That is a very quick way to NOT make a sale.

In fact, you're doing your prospect a disservice by giving them coaching at that point, because they will have a false sense that they can fix their problem on their own.

You and I both know that most people won't follow through on their own and they need your expertise and guidance to truly be successful with their health and wellness goals.

Heart-centered selling strikes a fine line between helping the prospect realize that the problem they have is big enough to solve now *and* big enough for them to invest in your program to achieve resolution. You can't do that if you're giving them a false sense that they can solve it on their own.

"You can't sell the store if you give away the candy." - My Mom

I've created an acronym to explain the full process of heart-centered selling, which I know will help you double your sales in the next six months. A bold claim, but one I'm confident making because not only did that happen for me, it's happened for the clients I've taken through this process.

In the following chapters, we'll go through the heart-centered approach in detail so you have not only context, but a process to follow to transform the way you sell your services.

H.E.A.R.T.

Hugs

This may seem a little silly, but I really believe in the need to make a connection with your prospects. One of the best ways to do this is by embracing them. 'Hugs' is all about rapport-building. When someone knows, likes and trusts you, the rest of the sales conversation goes much smoother. Not only that, it enables you to ask great questions to uncover the real problem.

Engagement

During this part of the process, you'll be asking engaging questions so not only you understand the problem your prospect has, but also allow the prospect to better understand their own problem. Do this, and they are more likely to make a change. It's one thing to tell someone they have a problem and another to get them to tell themselves they have a problem — the latter being much more powerful.

Ask

The 'ask' is typically referred to as the close — or simply asking for the sale. However, I believe the salesperson should never have to ask. The intention in heart-based selling is that the prospect becomes motivated and drawn by the conversation to ask YOU to help them.

Referral

Initially, you may think that referrals don't belong in a sales process. However, when you follow my process and get great results for your new client, an ask for a referral is definitely warranted and will be enthusiastically given.

Testimonial

Asking for testimonials is often overlooked, yet, social proof is what takes a cold prospect and turns them into a hot prospect. When your prospects see and hear what others are saying about you and the way you've transformed others' lives, they will be compelled to enroll in your program. It's essential that testimonial gathering become a consistent part of your practice.

That is the HEART approach to selling in a nutshell. Now, let's dive into each of these in detail.

FREE BONUS MATERIALS

If you want to go a bit deeper and further solidify your learning, I've put together a companion video course to go along with this book, along with some goodies to help you put what you learn into action.

Simply go to **www.TomJackobs.com/book/training** it's free to use, and my way of building trust in me.

You can also scan this QR Code:

Section 2: HUGS

Trust is the glue of life. It's the most essential ingredient in effective communication. It's the foundational principle that holds all relationships.

– Stephen Covey

Chapter 3

Building Trust with Integrity

There are salespeople who view all situations as a fight to the end and will do whatever possible to make the sale. We often think about car salespeople who just want the car deal that one time. This is an aggressive and transactional mindset. It also doesn't lend itself to creating a bond with a prospect that will not only garner an initial sale, but create a lifetime relationship.

It doesn't matter what industry you're in, every prospect and client is a potential REPEAT customer. If you're not treating every transaction as a building block to a long-term relationship, you're going to be leaving a ton of money on the table.

Sales should be the long game, not just a one-off transaction.

And that relationship starts with 'hugs'.

You know the feeling when you get a really nice embrace from someone? It feels comforting and you feel safe. This is how the beginning of any sales conversation should start. We need our prospect to feel comfortable and safe, otherwise they won't be willing to share the true feelings that drove them to contact you.

When prospects feel the sales consultation is more of a casual chat than a hard-pressure sale, and when the salesperson wants to create a long-term relationship, the sales process becomes easier and easier.

Hugs don't necessarily start when the client sits down in front of you for the first time, rather, this part should be inserted into all of your marketing. The prospect should already begin to know you and like you before you have the sales conversation. They should begin to feel comfortable with you and have a fairly good understanding of how you will help.

Hugs set the stage for your long term success as a salesperson and business owner. When you sell and deliver your services with integrity, you will increase the lifetime value of a client.

"Before working with Tom my close rate was just 30% and after just a month it went to 77%. Having an expert like Tom guide and coach me was invaluable to my success."

- Dr. Nick Belden, DC

As a seasoned sales coach and expert in health and wellness sales, I've seen how prioritizing the long game over quick wins can lead to exponential growth and sustainable success. Salespeople need to realize that their approach to each transaction can either open the door to a long and prosperous relationship, or slam it shut, potentially losing a valuable customer forever.

Integrity comes in many forms and is a recipe for long-term success.

1) Integrity to offer services that will definitely help people. If you're just looking to scam people or get a quick buck, then you will always be in hustle mode to get more prospects.

2) Integrity to say no when you can't help someone. It's powerful to be able to tell someone, "I'm sorry, I don't think I can help you with this issue." Or if you feel the person wouldn't use your program correctly, politely denying them the opportunity to purchase can also be very empowering as a salesperson (and show your integrity).

3) Integrity to provide the highest quality of service to your client. When clients are getting what they need AND MORE from you, they will be raving fans for life. Strive to create raving fans at every opportunity.

It can be a slow process, but the long-term rewards are very much worth holding on to your integrity, especially in the hard times. This will also enable you to increase the lifetime value of your clients.

What is lifetime value?

It's the revenue generated from a client over the life of the relationship.

If all you do is sell a four-week program and then have nothing after that, the lifetime value would be relatively low.

However, if you build a program that has a long-term approach or even includes consumable products, the lifetime value will increase.

There are only three levers you can use to increase your revenue.

1) Increase the number of leads and convert them to sales

2) Increase your prices

3) Increase the spend per client over their lifetime

Increasing the spend per client (lifetime value) is the easiest of all three since you already have that client and it's easier to sell to an existing client than it is to attract, educate and sell a new client.

With that said, we first address the conversion of new leads to clients with my heart-centered sales system. Nothing starts without the sale. If you have 10 leads per month and only convert two of them into clients, then there is definitely a conversion issue. And if you don't have a client in the first place, then you can't have a lifetime value.

When you have a firm sales process in place and understand that sales is all about identifying and solving your prospects' problems, you will double that conversion to four sales out of 10 prospects. You'll then be on the road to building a business and long-term success.

Hugs is where it all begins, and should not be overlooked.

"Integrity is doing the right thing, even when no one is watching." - C.S. Lewis

---

FREE BONUS MATERIALS

If you want to go a bit deeper and further solidify your learning, I've put together a companion video course to go along with this book, along with some goodies to help you put what you learn into action.

Simply go to www.TomJackobs.com/book/training it's free to use, and my way of building trust in me.

You can also scan this QR Code:

Chapter 4

Hugs In Practice

C an you identify the first time a prospect hears about you? It could be a social media post, an advertisement, a referral from a friend or even a talk you gave at their workplace.

It rarely is when they sit down in front of you (either physically or online) for the sales conversation.

How you market is how the relationship starts with your prospective new client. And your personality must come through. Since we can't help everyone and not everyone is our ideal client, we must present ourselves in a way that self-selects the type of clients we want to have.

The second touch point after your marketing efforts is when the prospect is scheduled for their initial appointment. During this scheduling call or automation, it's critical that you have a few qualifying questions to make sure the prospect is a great fit for you and you're actually able to help them.

When you ultimately have that sales conversation, whether in person, over the phone or on a video call, you are fairly certain that you can help them AND they are willing to accept that help.

Each one of these interactions should take H.U.G.S. into account. (And yes, that's an acronym as well.)

H - Honesty: Establish trust by being transparent and truthful in your interactions.

U - Understanding: Take the time to listen actively and empathize with the prospect's needs and concerns.

G - Genuine Interest: Show a sincere interest in the prospect's unique challenges.

S - Solutions-Oriented: Focus on providing valuable solutions that address their specific problems or goals.

With H.U.G.S. in your pocket, you've now set the stage for a very effective conversation that is sure to lead to a new client, and a client whose lifetime value with you will be high.

FREE BONUS MATERIALS

If you want to go a bit deeper and further solidify your learning, I've put together a companion video course to go along with this book, along with some goodies to help you put what you learn into action.

Simply go to **www.TomJackobs.com/book/training** it's free to use, and my way of building trust in me.

You can also scan this QR Code:

Section 3: Engage

"We have two ears and one mouth... use them proportionately"

- Epictetus

Chapter 5

Empathy and Active Listening

"The success of your sales will be determined by how much you listen." - Tom Jackobs

---

Empathy and active listening are the two top skills any successful salesperson must have. This is even more important when you are a H.E.A.R.T.-centered salesperson.

When you bring Empathy into the formula, you'll be unstoppable.

Empathy /empeTHē - the ability to understand and share the feelings of another.

When you have empathy for what the prospect is saying, you show that you truly care about them and genuinely want to help them fix their problem. When you are actively listening to what the prospect is saying, you will be able to respond empathically with statements and responses that connect with what they have to say.

There is nothing worse than feeling that the person you're speaking to isn't LISTENING to what you're saying. If your prospect feels this way (whether it's true or not), you will not make the sale.

One example is when you ask your prospect why their goals are important to them, and they respond with a sad story about how they're not able to play with their kids because they are fatigued all the time.

If you respond with a blanket, "Ok great," then move on to the next question, your prospect will feel as though they are in an interrogation and being asked questions by an uncaring person just wanting to make a sale. And I know that's not how you want to come across.

All you really need to do is respond to what they have said with simple statements showing that you are listening. One of the best ways of doing this is repeating back to them what they said in the form of a question, as if you're playing the game Jeopardy.

For example I would respond to this scenario with, "Oh my, so you're not able to play with your kids because of your fatigue?" and the tonality of my speech would be of a serious tone, which I call 'low and slow'. You go to a lower vocal range and slow down your speech.

This powerful psychological approach does two things for your prospect:

1. They will have to acknowledge your question, and they will thus hear the reason WHY they are looking for your help *again* — this time from you.

2. They will feel HEARD because you are repeating back what they said.

Try doing this in your normal conversations. You will find that the people you're speaking with will open up more to you and have a general feeling of closeness with you.

FREE BONUS MATERIALS

If you want to go a bit deeper and further solidify your learning, I've put together a companion video course to go along with this book, along with some goodies to help you put what you learn into action.

Simply go to **www.TomJackobs.com/book/training** it's free to use, and my way of building trust in me.

You can also scan this QR Code:

Chapter 6

Authenticity in Communication

During your sales conversation and especially during the ENGAGE part of the process, you will need to share some stories with the prospect.

Storytelling has been shown to create a deep connection between the teller and listener. Not only that ... everyone loves a good story that furthers a point.

Storytelling is a skill all business owners need to acquire. The great thing is that storytelling can be learned.

WHY... Why do you need to know how to tell a story?

Simple ... it's all about creating a connection with your prospect.

What you do and how you do it is important, but people will remember WHY you do it more when you tie it into your personal story.

Not only that, you will become more authentic with your communication. At the end of the day, we buy from other humans. Being that personal storyteller creates more momentum in the sales process, and your prospects will be more likely to buy from you as you build the emotional connection.

Do you need a tragic personal story or near death experience to have a good story?

No, not at all. What you do need is a way of crafting your story so it is engaging and conveys your message clearly.

Not only do you need to create your own personal story, but you should also create client stories as a way of showing how you're able to help your prospect solve their problem.

The basic structure in effective storytelling is:

1. **Impact moment**: What's the do or die moment in your story, when a decision needed to be made?

2. **Background**: What led up to that impact moment?

3. **Who or what helped you**: You are the hero in your story, so you need to have a guide to help you along the way. This could be a person, but it could also be a book, movie, thought or belief.

4. **Who or what hindered you**: Every good story has a villain. Just like the hero, it doesn't need to be a person, it could be a thought or belief or other force trying to keep you from reaching your goal.

5. **How you overcame**: What did you do to overcome the obstacles and ultimately get to your goal?

6. **What you learned**: How is life different now that the goal was achieved?

Here's an example of one of my signature stories.

Have you ever had a dream that was literally ripped out of your hands, thrown to the ground and stomped on?

That's what happened in July, 2008 when I competed in my first bodybuilding competition — or should I say — TRIED to compete.

In January of that same year, I decided to compete in a bodybuilding competition, primarily to: 1) see if I could do it, and 2) get six-pack abs.

I spent seven months working out, eating my prescribed meals, and sacrificing going out to dinner with friends in fear of messing up my progress. I even had to learn how to pose and have my poses choreographed to music. My choice was Dream On, by Aerosmith.

On the day of the judging, there I was … nervous, yet confident.

I checked in at 8:00 a.m. and was told that the morning pre-judging would be at 11:00 a.m. for the novice lightweight class.

PERFECT! I had time to do some final prep and get into my "flow."

I went out to my car in the parking lot to go over the music and the routine.

At 10:00 a.m., I went back into the auditorium to watch the other classes be judged. And that's when it happened.

I was looking at the guys on stage, and they looked really familiar.

And my stomach dropped.

That was the novice lightweights being judged on stage. It was where I needed to be.

The organizers had changed the time of my class' prejudging from 11:00 a.m. to earlier, and I didn't hear the announcement they made about the time change!

I frantically ran backstage, ripping off my clothes as I went.

The handler stopped me, "Number 53? Sorry man, you're disqualified."

To say I was crushed would be an understatement.

And to make matters worse, my parents flew from Cincinnati to Houston, and my two brothers came in from Cleveland and Los Angeles to cheer me on … but now there was no cheering to be done.

When I told my family in the parking lot, I was a massive wreck. I apologized to them for failing so badly.

My dad, a very stoic man, put his arms around me and said, "Son, you didn't fail us, just pick up the pieces and carry on."

And carry on I did.

After stopping at Starbucks for a Caramel Frappachino. I put on the routine for my family in my living room.

I called my coach and told her I'd be doing the next event in October and that I'd be back in the gym on Monday to continue my training.

And in October, I competed, this time planting my butt back stage and not leaving the building.

And I won first place.

This story can be used in many different ways. I can make a connection to sales coaching, to business and health.

Many prospects will automatically put you up on a pedestal and even be a little intimidated by you. The power behind a great story is that it serves to humanize you and make you relatable to your prospect.

In my opinion, you want to be the authority *and* also relatable and human in any sales setting. Crafting your personal story will do just that.

If you'd like the framework I use to work with clients one-on-one, helping them craft their personal stories, you can visit www.TomJackobs.com/storybook and download the exact method to craft your personal story.

FREE BONUS MATERIALS

If you want to go a bit deeper and further solidify your learning, I've put together a companion video course to go along with this book, along with some goodies to help you put what you learn into action.

Simply go to **www.TomJackobs.com/book/training** it's free to use, and my way of building trust in me.

You can also scan this QR Code:

Chapter 7

Solutions–Based Selling

"When there is no problem, there is no solution and therefore no sale." – Tom Jackobs

---

Heart-centered selling is all about uncovering your prospects' problem and then presenting your solution to solving that problem.

The issue that most health and wellness practitioners face is not digging deep enough during the sales conversation to allow the prospect to realize they have a problem big enough to warrant an investment in fixing it.

Many just rely on only explaining **how** they get great results for their clients, which will only get you so far in sales. Most people don't really care about the *how*, they want to have certainty that their problem will be SOLVED, once and for all.

If your prospect doesn't realize they have a big enough problem to be fixed, they won't proceed with the purchase.

How do we get to the problem and help the prospect realize it's of a magnitude that needs to be solved right NOW?

With the quality of the questions you ask.

I follow a very simple framework to uncover what the problem is.

It's important to note that these questions are more for the prospect than for you. Many prospects may not realize what the true problem is. Asking these questions — in this order — forces them to *hear themselves say that they have a big problem that needs to be solved NOW.*

This is an extremely important point worth repeating.

Your questions are more for the prospect to hear themselves say they have a problem, and secondarily for you to understand the problem so you can customize your presentation of the solution.

You could certainly **tell** the prospect what problems they are facing, but they may not believe you, since they may see you as a salesperson who just wants to make the sale. However, we generally believe the words we speak about ourselves. Therefore, we must have prospects tell us *and* themselves they have a problem worth solving *now*.

The **What Why What Why**™ Framework

The above framework encapsulates the only questions you need to ask to uncover the problem and establish the need to solve that problem now with the prospect.

Yes! It really is that simple.

Selling isn't complicated.

When going into the ENGAGE phase of the sales conversation you'll be asking these questions in this specific order.

WHAT #1: Establish The Desired Outcome

What are your goals? or

What is the outcome you want to achieve? or

What do you want to achieve by working with me?

The first WHAT question is designed to uncover where the prospect wants to get to — their destination. Without a destination in mind, there won't be a clear roadmap for getting to the destination.

Like going on a trip, you need to know where you're going or you'll just go around in circles and never get to where you want.

Sometimes, even though the prospect knows what they want, you may need to drill into the goal a little more.

This also establishes the "pleasure" state they want to be in once their problem is solved.

A secondary question which is good to ask at this point is, "What would it feel like to finally achieve that goal?" This gets the dopamine rushing in their brain as they start to see the end result of fixing their problem.

WHY #1: Uncover The DRIVER behind getting to the goal.

WHY is it important for you to fix this problem and get to the goal?

Of these four main questions, this one is the most important, so don't rush over uncovering the answer, and go deep.

This first WHY question establishes their motivation for fixing the problem. You will need to dig deep to get to the *emotional reason* for the prospect to get out of the "pain" they're in and finally get to the "pleasure" they are seeking.

People are much more motivated to get out of pain than they are to get to pleasure.

Imagine this scenario in your own life.

If someone stole $1,000 from you, how motivated would you be to get that $1,000 back?

Personally, I would go to the end of the earth to get that money back. Heck, I've done that and more for less.

Quick story: I was on a budget airline, you know the type … where they charge you extra for the seatbelt. I won't name names, but it starts with S and ends with COOT. I ordered a beer from the flight attendant, and when they went to charge my card, they were having issues with their card machine. So, they tried again (and then once more for good measure) before it went through.

When I looked at my card statement, I had been charged $6 (yes, $6 for a beer!) three times. I spent wayyyy too much time trying to get a refund, calling, emailing and even filing a claim with my credit card company to get the money back. Yes … all that work for just $12. I justified it with the, "It's the principle," theory.

On the flip side, I received emails asking for my opinion on the airline's services, where they offered a $25 gift card to complete the survey (which might've taken all of 10 minutes). And yet, I said to myself, "Ten minutes for $25 … not worth it!"

Perhaps you've had a similar experience, where you fought like hell to get something back, and are more blasé about gaining something "extra."

It's human nature, and you must understand that deeply in sales.

People are more likely to get out of pain (that's the push) than they are to get to pleasure (that's the pull).

When you can tap into both of those emotions, you are most certainly going to make a sale.

Push them out of the pain they are in and pull them to the pleasure they desire with their own emotions.

That is why this second question is so critical to dig deep and uncover the real motivation to get out of the pain. It gets the prospect to sit in that pain while at the same time dreaming about getting to the pleasure.

This second question will need some drilling into, to fully establish the emotional reason for them reaching that goal.

Many times, the first answer is just a surface-level answer. So dig, peel back the onion, and get to the emotional reason the prospect wants to get out of their pain and to their pleasure.

A sample follow up question:

Why else is it important for you to reach that goal?

Then keep repeating, "why else" until you feel you get some really good, emotional answers.

WHAT #2: Discover the history of failed attempts.

WHAT have you tried in the past or are you trying now to solve the problem?

Our second 'What' question does a few things for you and the prospect in helping them choose to work with you.

First, you help them realize they've been trying to solve their problem for a long time without actually achieving it.

Second, you will see a pattern of them spending a lot of time and money trying to solve their problem without actually getting to the root cause and fixing it.

With those two points established, you'll know if you can help them with your program. If you can't, you should end the conversation at this point and refer them to another solution.

You'll want to get an exhaustive list of everything they've tried, how long it took them, the outcome and the total cost of each failed solution.

When I was selling weight loss and fitness solutions, I always used this question to establish a patterned timeframe of how long they would try something, get a result and then revert back to where they were. Most people go through this yo-yo type of try-fix-fail cycle multiple times, thinking those solutions worked, when in reality — they didn't because they are back at where they started (or, oftentimes, worse off).

When you can help the prospect realize that all of this effort was in vain and they should actually be looking for a long-term, permanent solution, you will help them for a lifetime. How amazing would that be?!

This question also helps you when it comes to any price resistance. Most likely they've spent much more on all of the 'solutions' they've tried in the past than they would on the investment in your program. When you can help them realize that, you'll not only get a sale — you'll have a raving fan for life.

WHY #2: Create urgency to solve the problem now.

WHY is NOW the right time to make a change?

The second 'Why' question helps the prospect realize they need to get this problem solved now, rather than later. Urgency is a critical pathway to sales success.

Have you ever heard, "Let me think about it?" That is the worst objection ever. And it gives you some really good information. Specifically, you need to establish more urgency. When the prospect says this, it's never about the time to think about it, they just don't see the urgency to fix the problem now.

The pain isn't great enough, the pleasure isn't visible to them, and they are willing to just stay where they're at because it's "comfortable." Change is not comfortable.

Like the frog in a pot of water being slowly heated, they never try to jump out and eventually get cooked. Most people are content staying where they are unless there is urgency to change.

This is my favorite question because it gets the prospect to say they want to change through your program, *now* (as opposed to the typical sales approach wherein the salesperson TELLS the prospect why they need to buy the solution).

They won't believe YOU, because you have a bias to making the sale and every prospect knows what YOUR motivation is … it's to make a sale.

When the prospect tells YOU why they need to make a change now, they are telling themselves simultaneously. We never intentionally lie to ourselves, so they will believe themselves when answering this question.

Once you've asked those four questions and dig deep into the emotion behind each answer, you'll have just made the sale.

The prospect typically makes the decision to buy during this part of the sales conversation, when you've followed this framework and dug deep.

As long as you don't screw up the rest of the conversation, you will have a new client!

FREE BONUS MATERIALS

If you want to go a bit deeper and further solidify your learning, I've put together a companion video course to go along with this book, along with some goodies to help you put what you learn into action.

Simply go to **www.TomJackobs.com/book/training** it's free to use, and my way of building trust in me.

You can also scan this QR Code:

Chapter 8

The Mirror

O ne of the best communication techniques is to repeat back what the prospect told you to clarify what you heard and ensure you have the proper understanding of what they meant. When you install this technique into the sales conversation, it is a potent way to secure a sale.

Here is why ...

People want to be heard and understood. By repeating back to them what you heard, you are showing the prospect that you heard them and understood what they said.

Not only that, they are hearing the problems *again* from you — as aforementioned. They have expressed the problem themselves and now they are hearing it again from you, further emphasizing the need to fix it now.

I call it "the mirror," because it is equivalent to looking at yourself in the mirror and getting the reflection back on the problem. You must not skip this part, AND you must get confirmation from the prospect that what you heard was correct.

When done correctly, you will get a resounding, "YES! That's exactly it."

Simply go back through the *What Why What Why*, in your own words, while focusing on the pain they are in, and touch upon the pleasure they are seeking. Here is a sample structure of mirroring back in action:

SAMPLE SCRIPT:

- *Let me make sure I understand what you have said, you are experiencing [**MAIN PAIN POINT**],*
- *and you ultimately want to achieve [**GOAL/PLEASURE**],*
- *you've tried [**WHAT THEY'VE TRIED IN THE PAST TO CORRECT THE PROBLEM**],*
- *and have failed to reach [**THEIR GOAL**],*
- *not only that, but you want to fix this problem NOW rather than LATER because [**WHY THEY NEED TO DO THIS NOW**].*

And the prospect will go, "WOW! You totally understand what I'm going through!"

And you'll know you've just made a sale … but don't lose focus, you really need to solidify the sale in your presentation of WHAT you plan to do to help solve their problem, getting them out the pain they're in and ultimately to their goal.

By this point, you'll have all the information you need to create a customized presentation addressing all their concerns and eliminate objections so that they will make a decision on-the-spot to purchase your product or service.

FREE BONUS MATERIALS

If you want to go a bit deeper and further solidify your learning, I've put together a companion video course to go along with this book, along with some goodies to help you put what you learn into action.

Simply go to **www.TomJackobs.com/book/training** it's free to use, and my way of building trust in me.

You can also scan this QR Code:

Chapter 9

Presenting Your Solution

Now that you have all of the information you need from your prospect … AND you've confirmed you heard them correctly … it's time to present your solution.

If not done correctly, you will alienate the prospect and fail to make the sale, so be sure to take note of this point in the process.

Most practitioners haven't created a presentation that demonstrates how they help clients. It's in their head, and that is a mistake.

Showing a clear and concise pathway for eliminating the gap between where the prospect is and where they want to be is critical to making the sale.

Not only that, you also need to make sure you are addressing ALL of their concerns and potential objections to purchasing your program.

When creating presentations with my clients, I like to focus on the process or framework the prospect will go through to eliminate their problem and reach their goal. This will help the prospect see the steps, have confidence in the fact that there is a systemized (not haphazard) process in place, and ultimately see themselves succeeding.

This presentation is a short, concise visualization of your solution process — one that gives the prospect confidence in you and does not bore them to tears.

Once you have created your standard presentation giving a clear, step-by-step guide to solving their problem, then you must customize the presentation to the prospect so they see themselves moving from pain to pleasure.

As an example, I'll use the presentation for my Selling With H.E.A.R.T. Sales Program. If you're ever on a sales call with me, you will hear a version of this presentation customized to you.

My Selling With H.E.A.R.T. Sales Program is broken down into three distinct areas to help you get out of the rut you're in with your sales and get you to closing a majority of the prospects you speak to.

I do this by focusing on the Three P's: presentation, performance and profits.

As you stated earlier, you feel like your sales are "all over the place," and you don't have a concise way of speaking to prospects. That is due to not having a firm presentation in place. So, the first thing we'll work on is crafting a killer sales presentation and process so that you will close more deals.

Now, it's great to have a killer presentation and process, however, if you don't deliver it in the right way, your prospects won't want to purchase. This is why we then work on your "performance." And no, you don't need to be an actor to perform. This is just my way of helping you deliver the sales consultations in a way so your prospects will engage with you and ultimately purchase your service. We'll do role plays and

I'll review real live sales presentations you have and give you feedback on what you're doing well and what you need to improve on.

Finally, we work on profits — making sure you're consistently following up with leads and handling the administrative work efficiently. You know when I asked you what your close rate is and you didn't know off the top of your head? Well, that's a big problem because we can't manage what we don't measure. So, we're going to get some tracking and automation in place to make this easy for you so that you can ultimately spend more time making sales and less time on administrative things.

And that's basically the presentation.

I explain WHAT we'll be doing, connecting it to the pain and pleasure gathered during the WHAT WHY WHAT WHY™ questions, and show that there is a firm process we go through. It is also important to note that I'm not teaching at this point or going into exact details — that's not the purpose of the presentation. At this stage, you want to show that you're confident you can solve their problem and how your process will solve your prospect's pain and get them to their goal.

FREE BONUS MATERIALS

If you want to go a bit deeper and further solidify your learning, I've put together a companion video course to go along with this book, along with some goodies to help you put what you learn into action.

Simply go to **www.TomJackobs.com/book/training** it's free to use, and my way of building trust in me.

You can also scan this QR Code:

Section 4: ASK

"Ask and you shall receive" - Matthew 7:7

Chapter 10

The Art of Non-Pushy Persuasion

Most H.E.A.R.T.-centered salespeople I work with are ultimately coaches. The sales process is no different than coaching an existing client to the result they want. In the sales process, you're coaching the prospect to purchase your program so you can help them solve the problem they are facing.

There can't be a higher calling than that.

When you approach the sales process as a way of helping prospects and honestly knowing you are the best solution to their problem in your heart, you will never come across as pushy.

You should be confident and assertive — that doesn't mean pushy.

To me, a pushy salesperson is only interested in making the sale, as opposed to a heart-centered salesperson who is more interested in helping the prospect solve their problem.

Your prospect will know and feel the difference.

Focusing on the solution, not the sale, will keep you focused.

Your confidence in your ability to solve their problem will be contagious and transfer to the prospect.

Your empathy for the pain they are in will establish the trust needed to help them purchase your program.

Your ability to express even more concern about the pain they are in will help them realize they need to solve the problem NOW — not later.

I don't believe I've ever been accused of being pushy with a prospect. If anything, I've been thanked for helping them solve the problem before it got worse.

If a prospect were ever to say to me, "I feel like you're pushing me to do this," I would simply respond with, "Oh my gosh, I'm sorry if that is what you're feeling, it is not my intention to be pushy. I'm just very concerned with where you are right now and what lies ahead if you don't fix the situation you're in. Help me understand what you believe will happen if you don't fix this issue? What would your life look like six months from now?"

Do you see how you can turn the feeling of "pushy" into a feeling of concern?

This is assertiveness without pushiness.

This is selling from the heart.

This is real care.

When you are able to truly care about your prospects' well-being along with your ability to help them solve the pain they are in, you will not feel like you are pushing your product ON them, but rather, *allowing* them to purchase your program.

When you truly believe you can help someone overcome a problem they have, isn't it your obligation to do whatever you can to help them make the decision to work with you?

You will know you have done your job correctly when you don't even need to ASK the prospect to purchase.

FREE BONUS MATERIALS

If you want to go a bit deeper and further solidify your learning, I've put together a companion video course to go along with this book, along with some goodies to help you put what you learn into action.

Simply go to **www.TomJackobs.com/book/training** it's free to use, and my way of building trust in me.

You can also scan this QR Code:

Chapter 11

Handling Objections with Grace

"Objections are just clarifying questions. Don't fear them!" -
Tom Jackobs

I truly believe that when you have gone through the entire sales process and fully helped the prospect realize they have a big enough problem that needs to be solved now, you will not have objections.

However, sometimes you will get some clarifying questions.

I use a very simple framework for overcoming objections. When used properly, they will overcome the objection with grace and move the prospect towards the purchase.

Step 1: Acknowledge What You Heard

Some may feel like this is agreeing with the objection, however, it is not. You are merely acknowledging what you heard. You can simply say, "I understand" or, "I hear you."

It's important that the prospect feels heard and understood and that you're not just ignoring their question … or worse … dodging their question like a seasoned politician.

Step 2: Question the Objection

A very simple technique is to simply repeat the objection in the form of a question.

The prospect may say, "I think it's too expensive."

Your response can be as simple as, "You think it's too expensive?"

This will get your prospect to actually question their own objection. For a price objection I will often add, "Compared to what?" Again, this is to get the prospect to think about what they said and start to question, is it *really* too expensive?

Step 3: Blow the Objection Out of the Water

In order to obliterate the objection you need to use a combination of emotion and logic. When you've done your questioning and discovery phase correctly, you will have plenty of ammunition to completely destroy the objection and move the prospect closer to the purchase they need to make to solve their long-standing problem.

It may sound like, "Earlier when we were speaking, you mentioned that you tried to solve this problem by doing, x y and z, yet — it didn't solve the problem. When you combine the time and expense of doing all of those things and still not getting the result you want, would you say those activities were too expensive as well?"

Wait for their response, which will most likely be something along the lines of, "Yeah, I did spend a lot on those, but this seems like it is more than I'm willing to spend."

Then, you can move them to an emotional response with, "I totally understand that. Tell me, how would it feel when you finally get to the result you're wanting and get out of this roller coaster you've been on for the last *XX* years?"

Keep them focused on the fact they are still in the pain and haven't yet reached the goal because they haven't invested in the right program ... your program.

Step 4: Close The Sale

This is the step often skipped by amateur salespeople ... but you're not amateur now, so you'll finalize the objection handling with a very elegant manner of closing.

"Why don't we go ahead and get you on the road to [the goal they want] and finally fix [the pain they're in]?"

When you really care about helping your prospect, every tactic you employ to help them make the decision to work with you comes from your heart, and your prospect will not only respect you, they'll also know you care.

FREE BONUS MATERIALS

If you want to go a bit deeper and further solidify your learning, I've put together a companion video course to go along with this book, along with some goodies to help you put what you learn into action.

Simply go to **www.TomJackobs.com/book/training** it's free to use, and my way of building trust in me.

You can also scan this QR Code:

Section 5: Referrals

People influence people. Nothing influences people more than a recommendation from a trusted friend. A trusted referral influences people more than the best broadcast message. A trusted referral is the Holy Grail of advertising.

– Mark Zuckerberg

Chapter 12

Scaling Your Practice The Easy Way

"Asking for a referral is a privilege."
- Tom Jackobs

Believe it or not, selling doesn't end when the prospect signs up for your service. That new client has now entrusted you with helping them achieve their dream outcome. It is now your duty to deliver on that promise.

I trust you have the ethics to provide a high level of service now that you've used the Selling With H.E.A.R.T. system to sign up that new client.

What a great compliment to the service you provide when the prospect refers a friend or relative to you as well.

That is why I say referrals are earned and asking for a referral is a privilege.

I remember when I joined a health club for the very first time. I was a sophomore in college and I joined Bally's Total Fitness. I recall sitting in the consultation room as the salesperson beat me over the head with the contract until I signed it (at least that's what it felt like). Finally, I signed up for two lifetime memberships (just kidding, but — again — that's what it felt like!).

After I signed the contract (and my life away), he pushed another piece of paper in front of me with 10 blank lines.

"Congratulations Tom, now I'm sure you have some friends who would love to work out as well, so it would really help me out if you could give me the names and phone numbers of 10 of your friends."

What the heck?!

I thought, "Do you really think I want to put one — let alone 10 — of my friends through what I just went through in this room with you?!"

He definitely didn't earn a referral … and now that Bally's is no longer in business, I suspect many other people felt the same way.

So, when my first business coach told me I needed to ask for referrals in my fitness business, I started to break out in a cold sweat (I was triggered by the word *REFERRAL*).

So, I'm not going to suggest you ask for referrals right after you make a sale, you haven't earned it yet.

On the flip side, not a single one of your clients wakes up in the morning, looks at themselves in the mirror, admiring the transformation they just went through with your help and says to themselves, "I should really refer some people to you."

You have to ask.

And you have to ask at the right time.

And you have to ask in the right way.

The best time to ask for a referral is after your client has reached a milestone in their progress with you and emotions are running high.

The best way to ask is using a very simple script along with giving a great incentive for that referral.

Here's an example:

[CLIENT NAME] I'm so impressed with how you've [WHAT THEY HAVE ACCOMPLISHED SO FAR]. Have any of your friends or family noticed the change in you?

Let them answer

That's great! I'm not sure if you knew this or not, but we do have a referral rewards program. When you refer a friend to me, I give them $XXX off of their initial program as a gift from YOU, and when they sign up, I give YOU $XXX off your next bill.

And this is the key to getting more referrals for any business …

Here are three limited-edition referral cards worth $XXX each. Please hand these to those friends who have expressed interest in the transformation you've gone through. Can you do that to help them, and to help me help them?

The key here is to get plastic gift cards made up with the dollar amount the prospect would receive as a gift from their friend. There are lots of companies out there you can order plastic gift cards from.

And don't be cheap and get paper cards … they don't have the same effect as a plastic card. Plastic cards look and feel like credit cards and have intrinsic value because of it. Plus, you can recycle them when they come flooding back in from your happy clients.

Not One and Done!

Asking for referrals is not a one and done exercise. You must consistently ask to a point where your clients say, "Yes, I get it, you want a referral!"

You have the best marketing agency already in your business and it only costs you a few hundred dollars AFTER someone signs up! Talk about an amazing return on investment. Yet, it's probably the last marketing tactic we as business owners think of.

Set up this process, be consistent and persistent with the application of this tactic, and you'll have a nice flow of new prospects.

I had a doctor friend of mine who was one of my best referral partners because one of his patients told him how I helped him get his nutrition and exercise under control. I eventually got that client off of the cholesterol and high blood pressure medication my doctor friend was prescribing him.

I did the same referral program above with this doctor. I gave him dozens of gift cards that he, in turn, gave to his patients.

Whenever one of his patients came in for a consultation, they had the gift card in one hand and a credit card in the other and said, "Dr. Scraeder told me I needed to see you, how do I get started?"

It was the easiest sale ever.

And they were the best clients.

Implement this referral program and see your business easily multiply.

FREE BONUS MATERIALS

If you want to go a bit deeper and further solidify your learning, I've put together a companion video course to go along with this book, along with some goodies to help you put what you learn into action.

Simply go to **www.TomJackobs.com/book/training** it's free to use, and my way of building trust in me.

You can also scan this QR Code:

Section 6: Testimonials

"The proof is in the pudding!" - unknown

Chapter 13

Social Proof is King

I f you're not capturing testimonials from your existing clients, you are making your overall growth very difficult.

When a prospect sees your advertisements or organic social media posts, they are most likely going to look you up and see what type of program you have and the results you've been able to help others accomplish with your program.

If you don't have testimonials, then they won't know how good you are.

I also understand that it can be difficult to ask a client for a testimonial and not every client will want to give one. But that shouldn't stop you from trying, especially if you're serious about growing your business.

The best type of testimonial you can get is a live testimonial.

If you are giving a live presentation or putting on a seminar, with the intention of getting more clients, having an actual client get up and speak your praises is absolutely gold.

I used to run a women's-only fitness program in Houston. Every Saturday, we ran a "visitor's day." This was an open day wherein anyone could come and try the workout before signing up.

It was one of our best marketing efforts, since we could show off the program as well as our community of other like-minded women.

At the end of the workout, I'd invite all the prospects to a quick presentation about the program and the different membership options. I always had one of my existing clients say a few words. One client in particular, Kay, came to us when she was 50 pounds overweight, scared to go workout at a gym for fear of being judged, and not in the best of health. During her first three months, she had an amazing transformation — both physical and mentally. To say her testimonial was amazing would be an understatement.

This is how I would conduct the short presentation … take note and model it for yourself if you also do live events.

I'd first thank everyone for coming to the workout and ask them, "What did you like BEST about the workout?" Notice the wording here … it's very intentional. I didn't say, "What did you think about the workout?" I wanted to hear only positive comments to get everyone on the same page.

Then, I'd introduce the existing client to say a few words about her transformation. This is where the magic really happens, especially if you have a client like Kay.

Kay would tell the other ladies in the cutest southern accent, "I was a wreck when I first came here, I was scared to walk through the door my first time, my knees hurt, my back hurt and I was tired all of the time. That was just a short three months ago, now I have so much energy to play with my grandkids, my body doesn't ache all the time, AND I've lost 30 pounds in the process. Y'all would be stupid if you don't sign up right now!" **mic drop**

She said it from her heart and without any prompting from me.

Next, I'd go through the different packages we offered and hand out sign-up sheets. Super simple, yet so effective.

Needless to say, we always had a bunch of sign ups.

Think about the psychology of this process.

1. They just went through a great workout, feeling great and then …

2. They told me what they liked about it (while telling themselves at the same time), then …

3. They hear a client like Kay basically call them stupid if they didn't sign up!

How could you go wrong with that?

Aside from live testimonials, you must capture video testimonials. Videos are the next best thing because the words the person is saying are *their* words, in *their* voice and with *their* emotion behind them.

Video testimonials can be done over video conference or when the client is in the office. Just pull out your phone and record. Keep it simple!

You'll want to keep these less than three minutes long.

I suggest you ask three simple questions:

1. What was going on in your life that you decided you needed to seek help, and why did you choose my program?

2. What results have you achieved so far?

3. What would you tell someone in a similar situation who is thinking about joining this program?

Very simple and to the point.

And again, similar to referrals, asking for testimonials has to be a part of your process since no one wakes up and says, "I think I'll give Tom a testimonial today."

When asking a client for a testimonial, I use this very simple scripting.

[CLIENT NAME], you've been doing great and are really an inspiration. I'm sure your story would inspire others to take the action you have to resolve [THE PROBLEM]. Would you mind if I film a short CASE STUDY about your progress and results as a way of inspiring others to get the help you did?

I'm sure it would really help out a lot of people, plus you'd be doing me a huge favor as well so that I can help more people too.

When you frame the "testimonial" as a case study and a way of helping other people, how could someone say no?!

The last type of testimonial is the written testimonial. These aren't as strong unless they are screenshots of a post on social media or an actual review from Google or other review sites.

A friend of mine who runs a marketing agency has hundreds of testimonials, mostly video case studies. But he also asks his clients to post their results from his program in a private community group every week. Then he screenshots the results and uses those in his marketing, simply blurring out part of the name and picture of the client for privacy.

If you have a private community group, I highly suggest that you ask clients to post their results in the private group regularly as a way of keeping your clients accountable and celebrating their successes while also showcasing typical results IN THE WORDS OF THE CLIENT, in your marketing.

There you have it. Four different ways of collecting testimonials and how to use them in your marketing.

When you have tons of testimonials, prospects will come to the sales conversation fairly well convinced you can help them based on who you've helped previously … making your sales conversation exponentially easier.

My challenge to you is to set a goal of getting at least two video testimonials a month so that at the end of the year, you'll have twenty-four and be well on your way to making your sales and marketing efforts easier.

FREE BONUS MATERIALS

If you want to go a bit deeper and further solidify your learning, I've put together a companion video course to go along with this book, along with some goodies to help you put what you learn into action.

Simply go to **www.TomJackobs.com/book/training** it's free to use, and my way of building trust in me.

You can also scan this QR Code:

Section 7: Wrapping It Up

"We are what we repeatedly do. Excellence, then, is not an act, but a habit" – Will Durant

---

Chapter 14

The Heart-Centered Sales Journey

"Sales is a process." - Tom Jackobs

When I first started selling fitness programs in 2008, I had no earthly idea what I was doing. I had a very bad mindset about selling and couldn't close a door!

I led with price, didn't understand what the prospect's needs were and left it in their hands whether to purchase or not. I thought, the more I spoke, the more I could convince someone to work with me.

Completely ass-backwards!

No wonder I almost went broke within six months of opening my business.

In writing this book, I don't want other heart-centered salespeople to go through the same struggle I went through. Basically, I'm taking my last 17 years of learning and implementing successful sales strategies and boiling it down into an easy-to-understand and implement process that ANYONE can repeat … and I'm specifically speaking to YOU!

It All Starts at the Inquiry

The way you interact with your prospects from the very beginning sets the stage for all of their interactions with you.

When you get back to any inquiries within 20 minutes, you're showing them you care about helping them fix their problem and get out of the pain they're in.

Alternatively, if you wait a day or two, you're telling the prospect they aren't that important to you and they will just have to suffer until you get around to responding to them. Not a good first impression.

FREE BONUS MATERIALS

If you want to go a bit deeper and further solidify your learning, I've put together a companion video course to go along with this book, along with some goodies to help you put what you learn into action.

Simply go to **www.TomJackobs.com/book/training** it's free to use, and my way of building trust in me.

You can also scan this QR Code:

Chapter 15

Heart-Centered Follow Ups

"Failing to follow up on leads and prospects should be a criminal offense!"

- Tom Jackobs

Nﾠone of what you've just learned matters if you don't have prospects sitting in front of you. I don't cover lead generation strategies — as there are plenty of resources available for doing that. That having been said, one piece many business owners miss is the follow up with leads to book consultations.

Several years ago when I first started my Business Lead Maximizer (www.BusinessLeadMaximizer.com) program, I conducted a study to see how many fitness businesses followed up with their leads.

The results were truly shocking to me.

I had my staff contact 100 fitness centers across the US. They simply filled out the information forms on the fitness center websites with their information, requesting an appointment. My goal was to see how many responded to our inquiry, how quickly they responded, and using which media.

Of the 100, only 23 responded.

Of those 23 who responded, only four responded by phone.

Of those four, the average response time was 36 hours … which means that *not a single one* reached out within 20 minutes (and we filled out the forms during normal business hours!). Also, none of these four made more than one attempt to reach out.

All of the 23 who responded did so using an autoresponder via email … and a few by text.

Only 1% responded multiple times by phone!

How much do most businesses spend on advertising and getting leads?

Upwards of $20 per lead. Why not just light all of those $20 bills on fire?

In my experience, businesses don't have a lead problem, they have a follow up problem. And that is precisely why I created my Business Lead Maximizer … to help these businesses follow up persistently and consistently with their leads.

After all, the lead REQUESTED INFORMATION OR AN APPOINTMENT.

And in the several years since, we've made over a million phone calls and booked tens of thousands of appointments for health and wellness providers. In our experience, it takes an average of 9.7 attempts to reach someone on the phone.

If your business is only calling one time, you're leaving a ton of money on the table.

People are in a constant state of "busy" (real or imagined), so you must do your best to reach out to them multiple times in order to help them solve their problem.

And yes, when you implement this persistent and consistent strategy I provide in my downloadable document, you will get the few snowflakes who will complain about the amount of follow up. My question to you is, are you going to allow a few people to dictate how you run your business? After all, they *did* opt in for your information and gave you their phone number. All they need to say is "stop" or "not interested," and you stop the follow up. No big deal … move on to the next person.

However, many offices I've worked with get that one complaint and stop their entire follow-up program. It's a shame that one person can dictate your success in helping others.

If you're worried about this, then a mindset shift is in order.

When the lead enters their details, they should be called immediately … within 10 minutes. You have three times more chance of booking an appointment when you connect with that lead immediately … before they forget about you and before they move on to the next person on Google.

I've put together a guide on how to implement my proprietary follow-up process we use everyday in my appointment setting service at Business Lead Maximizer. You can download it here: https://www.BusinessLeadMaximizer.com/Monday

Following up on leads is an essential part of your sales process as well as your overall marketing strategy. And it's your obligation to help the prospect realize they have a problem big enough to solve NOW, not tomorrow — but now!

I get it though, many practitioners don't have the bandwidth or staff to implement this type of follow-up process, so it may be necessary to outsource this service to us at www.BusinessLeadMaximizer.com, it's definitely less expensive than hiring a part-time employee, training them, implementing systems and managing the process.

The Sales Conversation

Once you book that lead for a sales conversation, you must follow a very simple conversation structure to ensure:

1) you CAN actually help them and

2) you allow your prospect to realize they have a problem that needs to be fixed NOW and that you're the best option for fixing that problem

Your entire sales conversation should be mostly you asking questions, with the prospect doing most of the speaking. Think of the 80/20 rule: 80% them and 20% you.

Or, consider what my mom says, "God gave you two ears and one mouth … use them proportionately!" So SHUT UP and let the prospect spill their guts.

So let's break down that process:

The Intro and Rapport Building

You'll want to, of course, put the prospect at ease and start off with a little small talk to warm up the conversation. The only caveat here is to not make this too long and drawn out, as it will be easy to detract from the goal of your conversation — to enroll your prospect.

Questioning and Info Gathering

This is the most important part of your conversation. This is also where the sale is made, believe it or not.

Earlier, I went through the ***What Why What Why*** framework, which will guide your questioning.

The key point to remember is that the questioning section is primarily for THE PROSPECT to hear themselves say they have a problem that needs to be solved NOW. Secondarily, you will have great information to be able to customize your presentation and highlight how your program will solve all of their problems, once and for all.

The Mirror

Great communication is all about understanding the other person. The best way to show you understand what your prospect said is to repeat back what you heard them say in your own words.

This will also allow the prospect to hear what their problem is and why they need to have it solved now and with you.

People want to know that you care, that you understand them, and that they've been heard. If it feels like you're just following a script, then they are less likely to feel that you understand their needs and are able to help them.

Do not skip this step!

Presentation

This is your opportunity to speak about how your program will be able to address your prospect's specific needs. The trap many salespeople fall into is they have a standard presentation they use for everyone. While having highlights on what you need to go over is a good thing, you MUST focus on the points that will help your prospect with their unique problem.

You do this by linking what they said in the questioning phase to how your program can solve those problems.

This will show your prospect you were listening and that your program can specifically help them get out of pain and get to their goal.

Customization is key.

Allow the Purchase

Some may say, "Close the sale." I prefer to say, "Allow the purchase." Again, at this point — if you've done the other sections properly — the prospect should be asking YOU, "How do I get started?" and reaching for their credit card.

One of the best ways I've found to allow for the purchase is to link the program to their goal and their desire to get out of pain.

You may want to say something like:

Based on what you've told me and in my expert opinion, you really need to go through my XYZ program to ultimately get to [THEIR DESIRED GOAL] so you can stop suffering with [BIGGEST PAIN POINT], ok?

The program is just $XXXX, and like you said, you want to get off this hamster wheel and finally achieve your goal, right?

At this point they will automatically agree with you.

And you can start the enrollment process.

I remember the first time I tried this with a prospect, like it was yesterday. Her name was Sharon. She walked into my fitness center for her consultation, I had my computer set up with the presentation and my list of questions to ask.

I went through each one of these steps and at the end I said, "Sharon, based on my expert opinion and having helped hundreds of people just like you achieve the results you want, I'd recommend my 100-session package, which is just $5,500. Now, you could possibly achieve that with the 50-session package, but to really solidify your results, I do recommend the 100 sessions. Which would you prefer?

I then shut my mouth … before I would have probably said something like, "Well, maybe try it first for free and see," (or something stupid like that) rather than allow Sharon to make a decision. You never know what is going on in their minds at this point. So just zip it up and allow them to make a decision.

Then, after what seemed like an eternity, She said, "Okay, let's do that," and handed me her credit card.

I think I may have actually said, "Are you sure?"

I had never sold a training package worth $5,500 before and honestly didn't think someone would buy it — even though I knew in my heart of hearts that she needed it to achieve the goals she wanted.

I also didn't know if my bank would even process a $5,500 charge!

To my surprise, it all went through and Sharon went on to be a client of mine for 5 years … think of the lifetime value of a client like that!

That is the basic Selling With H.E.A.R.T. Sales process. But, in case it doesn't go quite as planned, you may need to handle a few objections.

Objection Handling (Clarifying Questions)

Most salespeople panic when a prospect then asks some clarifying questions. This is why I don't like the phrase, "objection handling" — because they aren't always objections.

A question like, "Do I have to pay that up front?" is not an objection. They just want to clarify the payment program. So just respond, "That would be best."

A question like, "Do I need to make a decision now?" is also not an objection. They just need to clarify when to start. They didn't say they don't want to get started, they just want to know when. And of course, since they already told you in the questioning phase WHY they need to make a change now, you will have a ready answer from what they've already told you.

Like, "Well prospect, earlier you told me that you needed to make a change now because … so yes, now is the time to make that decision, which I think you've already made, right?"

FREE BONUS MATERIALS

If you want to go a bit deeper and further solidify your learning, I've put together a companion video course to go along with this book, along with some goodies to help you put what you learn into action.

Simply go to **www.TomJackobs.com/book/training** it's free to use, and my way of building trust in me.

You can also scan this QR Code:

Conclusion

When you put into practice all we have gone through with the Selling With H.E.A.R.T. Sales system, you will be well on your way to helping more people and having a thriving practice.

This book is meant to be a practical guide. You should refer back to sections in this book when you feel you are stuck or if your sales conversions take a dip.

What I have found in my own sales career and in coaching hundreds of business owners is that we all get lazy or bored with our process — EVEN WHEN IT'S WORKING PERFECTLY — and we want to mix it up a bit. I suggest you squash those urges and remember that sales is a PROCESS, and when you follow this sales process, you will get the same result over and over again ... more sales!

Remember, nothing happens in this world without a sale.

Next Steps

Congratulations, you now have in your head and heart a process to convert a lead into an appointment and ultimately a paying client with increasing lifetime value, complete with referral strategies and testimonials to get more clients FAST.

Not to mention, you are doing it with your heart and integrity intact.

Now, would you do me a solid favor and write a review of my book on Amazon? It would mean the world to me and help more heart-centered practitioners help more people.

If you know of anyone who could benefit from my book, why not get them a copy, or send them the link to purchase it on their own?

Don't forget to subscribe and listen to **The Heart-Led Business Show**, available on all major podcast platforms, where I feature heart-centered businesses and share their wisdom with practical advice you can implement in your own business.

https://podcast.HeartLedBusiness.show

About Tom Jackobs

With over 30 years of entrepreneurial roller coaster rides under his belt, Tom is basically a business veteran who's had more ups and downs than a yo-yo on caffeine.

While most folks might shy away from failure, Tom has embraced it like a long-lost friend. In fact, he's got so many failure stories, he's thinking of starting a Failures Anonymous group — but that's a whole different book.

In 2018, Tom waved a tearful goodbye to his beloved fitness business of 10 years and transformed himself into the Impact Pilot. His mission? Helping fellow entrepreneurs rake in more cash by sprinkling some sales strategy fairy dust and liberally using stories to sell. Tom's got the real magic wand here!

You might be wondering how a guy with a BFA Degree in Theatre from DePaul University ended up navigating the treacherous skies of entrepreneurship. Well, the truth is, Tom also has a private pilot license for single-engine airplanes, and he's here to prove that business can be just as thrilling as flying solo at 10,000 feet.

But Tom's talents don't stop there! He's been a contributor to CBS Radio, a guest on the Great Day Houston television show, Univision, Fox 26 News, KPRC Channel 2, The CW Houston, and a guest on more than 50 podcasts. Everywhere you look, there's Tom, dazzling the stage!

And if that's not enough, he's also a frequent speaker at industry events.

If you're interested in hiring Tom to speak at your next event, please reach out here: speaking@tomjackobs.com